Sticky Kitty

**Create a Miniature World of
Supercute Paper Cats!**

by Killigraph

This book is full of adorable cat silhouettes.
Let's find your favorites!

Welcome to a Miniature World of Sticky-Note Cutouts

Sticky notes are used every day in a variety of settings, like at the office, at home, or at school. Wouldn't you like to do something fun with them? Since sticky notes have low-tack glue on them, they can be reused any number of times. By cutting sticky notes into fun shapes, you can use them in all sorts of amusing ways: Decorate your room with them, arrange the cutouts as if they were on a stage and photograph them, adorn indoor plants with them, or use them as gift labels . . . whether practical or fanciful, the possibilities are limitless!

In this book, we introduce you to the joys of paper cat cutouts. Cats' charming and adorable behaviors have inspired the more than 10 unique crafts that make up this book. Miniature worlds will spring forth from your imagination. Let's give it a try!

We've made silhouettes of various breeds of cats.
Can you tell how many different cat breeds there are
just by looking at the silhouettes?

Let handmade sticky kitty crafts bring cuteness and joy to your home, parties, and loved ones!

Contents

Chapter 1

Sticky Kitties: Behaviors

Chapter 2

Sticky Kitties: Cat Breeds

Chapter 3

Handmade Cat Crafts

Kitties Demystified!

Materials and Tools

Sticky Notes
Sticky notes can be of any brand or type, but we recommend the 3-x-3-inch (75-x-75-mm) size. Refer to p. 11 for sticky-note types and materials.

Craft Knife
Use a craft knife that can make fine cuts and be maneuvered precisely for detailed shapes. We recommend a blade angle of 30 degrees.

Cutting Mat
Use a self-healing cutting mat that does not produce shavings. A small cutting mat from a craft store should suffice!

Patterns
Make photocopies of the patterns found at the end of this book and use them to make the cutouts. For those who find making lots of tiny cuts difficult, we recommend using enlarged photocopies of the patterns.

Optional Materials
The following items will come in handy for more elaborate projects: cardboard, cardstock, construction paper, double-sided tape, an eyeleteer (a small, pointed tool for making holes), glue tape (both low-tack and strong), origami paper, and a utility knife, which can be used to cut thicker paperstock, such as cardboard.

Sticky-Note Cutout Techniques

1.

Photocopy the pattern and place it on the sticky note

Make a full-size (or enlarged, if you want to practice on bigger cutouts first) photocopy of the cat patterns on pp. 82–93, and roughly cut out a pattern of your choice. Align the pedestal, or the rectangular area with the diagonal lines, with the adhesive part of the sticky note and press it down.

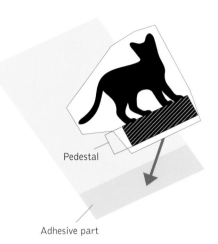

Pedestal

Adhesive part

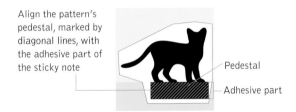

Align the pattern's pedestal, marked by diagonal lines, with the adhesive part of the sticky note

Pedestal

Adhesive part

2.

Cut out the pattern by tracing the outline

Hold the pattern down firmly with your fingers and trace the outline of the pattern using a craft knife. This task is easier if you cut the pattern starting from the top of the pedestal, near the adhesive part, and move toward the cat's upper body. Cut around the pedestal last.

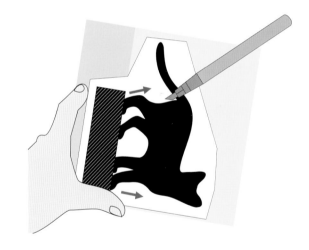

3.

Fold the pedestal to make a stand

Remove the pattern and stand the cat up by folding the pedestal at a 90-degree angle. Now you have your own sticky kitty, ready for action!

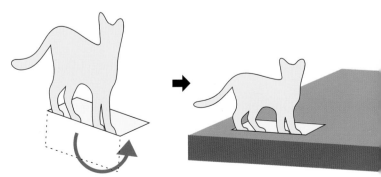

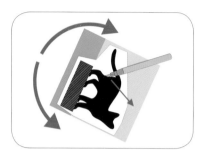

Tip
1.

Move the pattern around when cutting

When using the craft knife for cutting, pull it diagonally toward you in the direction of the hand holding the knife. For example, if you are right-handed, cut diagonally in the right-down direction. Hold the blade down and move the pattern around to cut out the shape of the cat.

Tip
2.

First cut out unnecessary parts

Start by cutting out inner areas that will be discarded. If you cut the outer frame first, cutting out the inner parts will be more difficult due to a less stable surface area. Similarly, cut out thin and long parts early on.

Tip
3.

Start cutting from sharp angles

For sharp angles, begin by cutting from inside the angle and carefully pull the knife outward.

Tip
4.

Check the back side to complete the cutout

After cutting out the pattern, flip the sticky note over and check the back to see whether it is fully cut through. If there are places that are still intact, trace the uncut parts from the back with a utility knife.

Standard Paper Sticky Notes

Sticky notes come in a variety of colors, sizes, and shapes. We recommend you outfit yourself with assorted packs of 3-x-3-inch (75-x-75-mm) squares, which is the size we use in this book. There are bright-color sets as well as fluorescent and pastel sets. If you get a multicolor pack in each of the three color categories, you'll have a generous selection of colors to work with. There are many brands to choose from, but we recommend Post-it, as they offer lots of different colors and a relatively strong adhesive glue.

Sticky notes come in multicolor packs, and the colors are usually grouped by category: bright, pastel, fluorescent, etc.

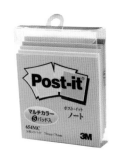

Sometimes you can find a designer series of specialty colors.

Film-Type Sticky Notes

For film-type sticky notes, we recommend those that come in 3-x-3-inch (75-x-75-mm) size. The vellum-like material makes sturdier cutouts than paper and offers a different visual effect.

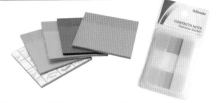 

Film-type sticky notes come in great colors.

Sticky notes can be found at office-supply, craft, and dollar stores.

Sticky Pockets

Wall pockets with flat pouches for holding papers can also be used for cutouts. The pockets have low-tack glue on them, just like sticky notes, but are made of durable film-type material. They come in vivid colors like red and pink, as well as monotone colors, such as black, gray, and white, which are not common colors for paper sticky notes.

Monotone pocket sticky notes allow you to make larger cutouts in more subdued colors.

Sticky-Note Tape Rolls

Sticky-Note Tape Rolls

Did you know that sticky notes also come in rolls? They feature the same low-tack glue and come in paper and film types. The tape rolls come in various widths, from ½ inch (15 mm) to 2 inches (50 mm). In this book we use the 1-inch (25-mm) product.

Full-Adhesive Roll

These roll-type sticky notes have strong adhesive glue. They can be attached to hard-to-stick places, such as coarse surfaces. We recommend this product when making wall stickers.

Cat Behaviors Explained

Part 1

Endearing Cat Gestures

Introducing adorable cat behaviors!

Looking at cats' various random poses and behaviors will surely make you even fonder of them. Kiyochan, whose blog "Dakara Tokyo ga Suki! Machi no Nekotachi" (The Reason I Love Tokyo! Cats Around Town), explains the reasons behind cat behaviors below. Whether they are strays or pets, the cats in these photos show off their spontaneous behaviors and adorable expressions. Let's appreciate the fascinating cat moments captured in these photos!

All that rolling around has a purpose

When a cat shows its stomach to people within arm's reach, it is a sign that he trusts them. A cat will certainly be pleased if you play with him when he bares his tummy. But if a cat shows the same behavior at a distance, he is telling himself to calm down, as he has started to panic. If you approach such a cat, he might jump and run away.

It's not just peeing, it's marking

Claiming territory is crucial for cats trying to obtain food. They use their own specific scent to mark their territory. By marking up high, cats tell others that they are big and strong.

Chapter 1
Sticky Kitties: Behaviors

Here are sticky-note cutouts of various cat poses and behaviors.

Try imagining their adorable actions when making your cutouts.

In this chapter, we have created a miniature world using paper cutouts,

alongside other items, like building blocks, toys, and dollhouse figurines.

You can use these pages as a reference when you take photographs of

your own paper-cutout creations.

OK, shall we go for a walk?

Oh, it's our neighbor.
I hope she feeds us.

We used black wall pockets to make our black cats.

See p. 11 for details.

Relaxing at home.

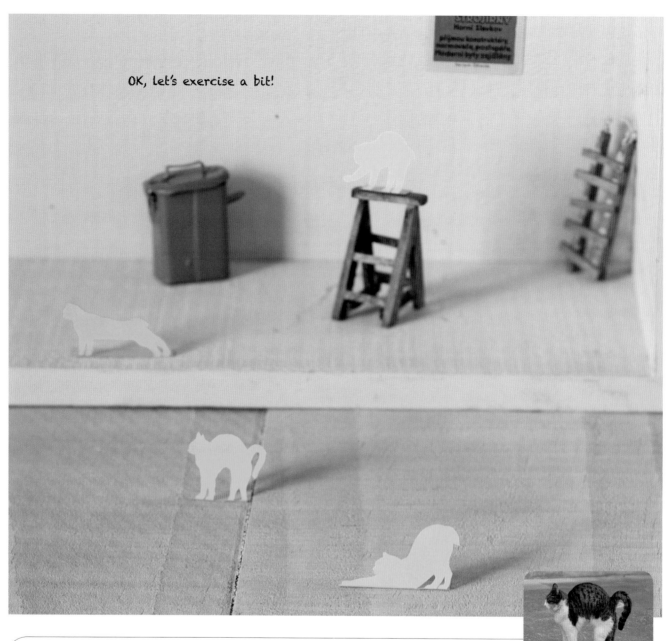

OK, let's exercise a bit!

Things Kitties Do **01**

Meoooow!

Stretch and shrink like an accordion

A cat's body is flexible, and daily exercise is essential to maintain top form. A big stretch after napping also helps cats wake up.

Rope-walking over flags of all nations!

Look, a chair!

How very cozy it looks!

Hey, I wanted to sit there . . . .

Oops, sorry.

Gather around, everyone!

Things Kitties Do 02

Sitting like this doesn't mean cats are sloppy

Cats sit deeply on their bottoms when they groom themselves. When they raise up their heads in the middle of this task, like in these photos, they look as if they're sitting sloppily.

Rolling around . . .
Ah, this feels good.

Things Kitties Do **03**

Grooming is not just for good looks

When cats lick themselves during grooming, it's not just to clean their bodies. It also helps them calm themselves down when they are feeling grumpy. So when cats are grooming, it's best to give them some space.

Huh?
Who are they?

And there are
so many of them....

Lick, lick....

Instagram Snap

Sticky Kitty Snapshots, Take 1

When you go to a coffee shop or a restaurant, take advantage of the surroundings by taking pictures of your cat cutouts. If you use smartphone applications like Instagram, you can upload your best shots to a social networking site, and share the supercuteness with everyone.

Cat Behaviors Explained

Part 2

Did you know that cats move their paws differently when they walk and when they run? Do you ever wonder what they're thinking when they're lazily rolling around?

Endearing Cat Gestures

What's the difference between walking and running?

Depending on their walking speed, cats may move their right front paw and right back paw at the same time or alternately. When they run quickly, their entire body works like a spring, and they can reach speeds of up to about 31 miles per hour (50 km/hour).

They may look bored . . . but they're relaxing

The cat in the picture at left is not lying still, waiting to pounce on her prey. She is relaxing. Maybe she's thinking, "Oh, I'm bored. I want some excitement." Her back paws also look relaxed.

Cats stay close together when they have special ties

Cats often stay close to one another, because that makes it easier for them to observe their surroundings. But they don't do this with just any other cat—only ones they trust. So cats that snuggle together are usually close blood relatives, like a parent and child or siblings. Cat families like to stay together.

Chapter 2

Sticky Kitties: Cat Breeds

There are many different breeds of cats, and each has a characteristic silhouette.

Let's start by cutting out the shape of your favorite breed!

In this chapter, we will show you how to make cat cutouts using regular nonsticky paper.

Then, you can combine these cutouts with objects from daily life,

place them in fun settings, and take pictures! You can use the photographs

in this chapter as a reference when you assemble your cutouts.

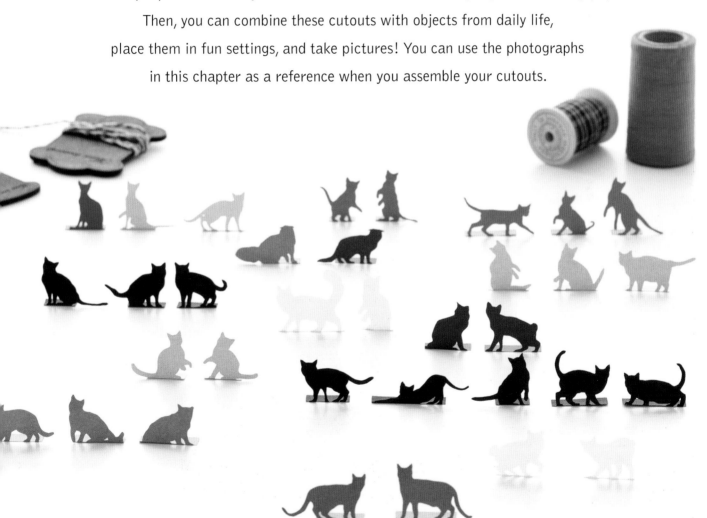

Making Cat Cutouts Using Nonsticky Paper

Because the colors of sticky notes are somewhat limited, you may want to use plain paper to make cat cutouts in dark shades like black, navy blue, and brown. Here's how to make fanciful cat cutouts using regular paper.

1

As with the sticky-note cutouts, make a photocopy of the cat patterns on pp. 82–93, and roughly cut out a pattern of your choice. Select a sheet of plain nonsticky paper and cut it in a size slightly larger than your pattern. In this book, we use origami paper.

Low-tack glue tape

2

Apply low-tack glue tape onto one edge of the paper in a single stroke. Do not repeat applying the glue onto the edge. It will make a mess!

3

Align the pattern's pedestal part with the edge where you applied the glue tape. Cut out the pattern with a craft knife by tracing the outline.

4

Gently remove the pattern. The pattern may stick to the cutout. Avoid this problem by placing a piece of magic transparent tape between the pattern and the cutout at the pedestal.

Recommended paper

Origami paper

Origami paper comes in a set of sheets in multiple solid colors or in a patterned design. The standard size is 6 x 6 inches (15 x 15 cm), which is what we use in this book. Origami paper can be found in craft stores. It has a weight similar to photocopy paper.

Recommended glue tape

Removable glue tape

This tape-style glue allows for uniform application of removable glue. Glue tape works better than glue. It comes in both low-tack and strong adhesions, so be sure to check the label. For making sticky kitties from nonsticky paper, we use low-tack glue for the pedestal. But we use the strong glue for other applications in this book.

Removable glue tape is easy to use and keeps your crafts tidy.

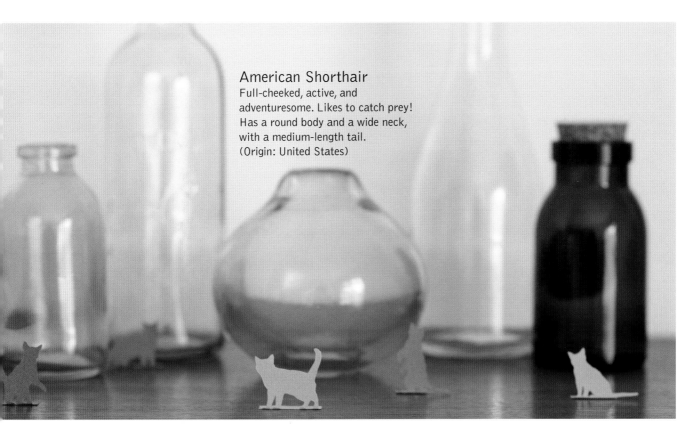

American Shorthair

Full-cheeked, active, and adventuresome. Likes to catch prey! Has a round body and a wide neck, with a medium-length tail.
(Origin: United States)

American Wirehair

Has wiry hair and curled whiskers. Friendly and active. Looks similar to the American shorthair.
(Origin: United States)

American Bobtail

Has a brawny body and a short, round tail. Quiet and social. Highly interested in shiny things.
(Origin: United States)

Japanese Bobtail

Has a lean and muscular body, with a round tail. Gentle and mild. Easily adapts to changes in environment. Model of the raised-paw "lucky cat" figurine placed in many Japanese shops to lure in customers. (Origin: Japan)

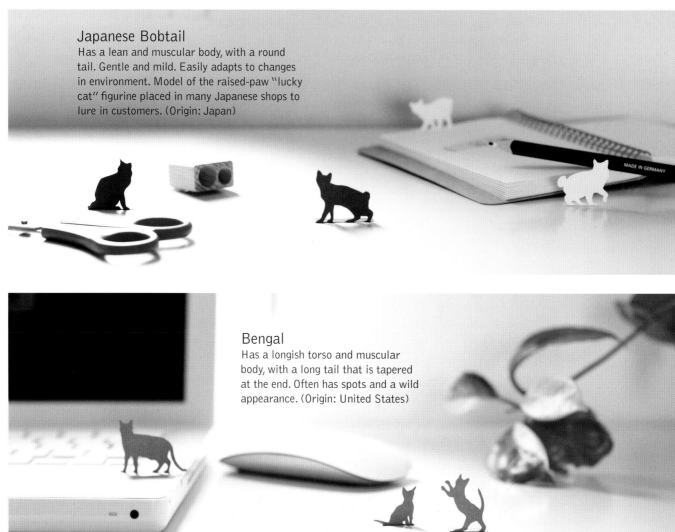

Bengal

Has a longish torso and muscular body, with a long tail that is tapered at the end. Often has spots and a wild appearance. (Origin: United States)

British Shorthair

Has a big, rounded face and small ears
that stand a bit apart. Body is stocky,
with relatively short paws. Has a hardy
appearance. (Origin: Britain)

Persian

Has big, round eyes and a snub nose, with a long and furry coat. Has short paws and a massive build. Gentle and able to cope with loneliness. (Origin: Britain)

Ocicat

Has a large, long, and well-balanced body, with features of a wildcat. Has a long, thin tail. Grows obedient to the master as it matures.
(Origin: United States)

Burmese
Has a rounded body and paws, with short hair. Easily adapts to new environments. Social and mischievous! (Origin: Thailand)

Scottish Fold
Has a midsize, roundish body but is muscular. Has cute, small drooping ears and a long tail. Mild and sweet-tempered. (Origin: Scotland)

Bombay

Has a muscular and solid body, with ears that are round at the tip. With its shiny black coat, it is the iconic image of the black cat. (Origin: United States)

Siberian

Having originated in an intensely cold land, it has a thick coat. Has a relatively large body. Clever and patient. (Origin: Russia)

Havana Brown
Slim with long paws. Taking after the Siamese, it has a slightly long face and big ears. Its tail is thin. Seeks affection and is playful. (Origin: Britain)

Exotic Shorthair
Looks like the Persian but with shorter hair. Has a robust body, with fat paws, a short tail, and small ears. Gentle and composed. (Origin: United States)

Ragamuffin
With a thick chest, it is a large cat that can weigh up to 22 pounds (10 kg). Has a fluffy tail that looks like a brush. Loves to be loved. (Origin: United States)

Norwegian Forest Cat

Has a thick coat to withstand the cold, with a gorgeous tail. Large-boned and stout. Mild and intelligent. (Origin: Norway)

Russian Blue

Has a slim body with a short, thick, fine, and silky coat. Its tail is relatively long and tapered at the end. Very cautious. (Origin: Russia)

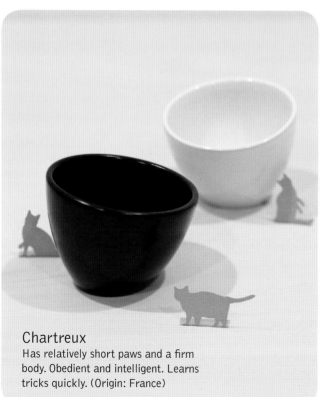

Chartreux

Has relatively short paws and a firm body. Obedient and intelligent. Learns tricks quickly. (Origin: France)

Ragdoll

A large cat with a long coat and husky body. The female is much smaller than the male. Calm, fearless, and gentle. (Origin: United States)

Oriental

Has a slim body with long and thin paws. Its face is also long and narrow, with a thin tail. Seeks attention. Somewhat nervous. (Origin: United States)

Film-type sticky notes are resistant to water, so they can be used to decorate houseplants!

 →  →  →

Cut plastic plant labels, which can be purchased at nurseries or home and garden stores, into shorter lengths.

Attach your cat cutout made from a film-type sticky note onto the shortened label. You can even add glue for a stronger adhesion.

If the pedestal of your cutout is wider than the plant label, cut the bottom of the cat's legs free from the pedestal in the protruding areas, then fold the outer pedestal part behind the label.

Stick the label into the planter to decorate it. Careful when watering, or your sticky kitty will get wet!

Cornish Rex

Has a slim body and long paws, with an egg-shaped head and large, cone-shaped ears. Has a great deal of curiosity. (Origin: Britain)

Birman

Has a relatively long torso, with a long coat and more space between the ears than other cats. Has a fluffy tail. Clever and emotionally stable. (Origin: Burma)

Turkish Angora

Has a flexible body with a fluffy tail. Its ears are relatively big and stand upright. It's social but has a low tolerance for stress. (Origin: Turkey)

Abyssinian

This breed is said to be the oldest among housecats. It has a slender build with long paws and tail. Has a great deal of curiosity but is somewhat skittish. (Origin: Britain)

Siamese
Has a thin and muscular body, with big, wide ears. Highly sensitive and picky, but clever. (Origin: Thailand)

Singapura
Has the smallest body among cats, with sharp ears, a round face, and a thin, long tail. It grows only to about 6 pounds (2.7 kg). Mischievous and active. (Origin: Singapore)

Maine Coon
With a sturdy body, it is a large breed with a long coat. Can grow as heavy as 22 pounds (10 kg). Daunting size aside, it's very relaxed and accommodating. (Origin: United States)

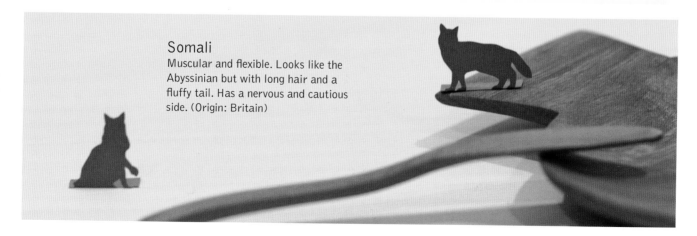

Somali
Muscular and flexible. Looks like the Abyssinian but with long hair and a fluffy tail. Has a nervous and cautious side. (Origin: Britain)

Instagram Snap

Sticky Kitty Snapshots, Take 2

Go outdoors and look for picturesque scenes in the park or around town where you can take pictures of your cat cutouts. Compared to indoor lighting, the light outdoors lends vivid color to your cutouts and backgrounds. It's also fun to try to capture your sticky kitties in what appears to be a cat-size world by experimenting with proportion and placement of your cutouts in different open-air settings. Be bold and playful!

Cat Behaviors Explained

Cats not only exhibit adorable behavior, they also have superb physical abilities. They have primal instincts even when they're sleeping!

Part 3

Endearing Cat Gestures

Cats hold their tail upright when they want attention

When cats hold their tail upright and approach you, it is a sign that they're seeking attention. They would love for you to pet them. When they bend the tip of their tail forward, they are greeting you with a friendly hello.

They jump so high!

Cats are said to be able to jump to a level about five times their height, and that's just a simple vertical jump. When they climb a tree, for example, they use their paws to thrust themselves upward so they can reach even higher places. Even with their little bodies, they can climb up high and stretch their paws long!

Cats are alert even when sleeping

Cats spend more than half the day sleeping. But it's not unusual for a cat that's napping in the sun to be gone the next moment. This is because of their primal instinct, which tells them that it's dangerous to stay in one place for a long time. Cats spend their days taking a short nap in one place and then moving on to a different place for another quick nap. That's where the word "catnap" came from!

Chapter 3

Handmade Cat Crafts

Cat-shaped sticky-note cutouts can be used to decorate rooms
and to adorn gifts. In this chapter, we'll give you some ideas for handmade crafts!

❤ Cat Craft 1

Cat House Envelopes

Here we've made stylized envelopes you can use for special letters. These are made from envelopes with a clear cellophane window. With some construction paper and a sticky kitty placed inside, it looks as if the cat is peeking through the window of his own house. How sweet is that?

Instructions → p.65

🐾 Cat Craft 2

Gift Bags

You put a present inside a gift bag, but then you want to add a little something to make it look attractive. This is when your sticky kitties will come in handy. You can use a decorative paper fastener or twist tie to turn the bland paper sack into a pretty gift bag. You can add on a used postage stamp, doily, or other embellishment to make it even cuter.

Instructions → p.65

Paper fasteners come in various shapes—try looking for some unique ones.

Make gift bags in all shapes, sizes, and colors!

❀ Cat Craft 3

Simple Garlands

This is a simple garland that combines triangular flags and sticky kitties. It can be used as interior decoration and is perfect for birthday parties and other celebrations. Enjoy matching each cat with your favorite decorative tape and patterned paper.

Instructions → p.66

You can also make labels for jars and bottles and attach them with thread. Add a cat cutout and some stickers, and then write a message on the label!

🐾 Cat Craft 4

Cat Hooks

Decorate your wall with business cards, your favorite postcards, or photos, using colorful sticky kitty cat hooks. Film-type sticky notes are sturdy and work well as hanging cat hooks.

Instructions → p.66

❀ Cat Craft 5

Sticky-Note Covers

Make a cover to help organize your sticky-note packs before some of them get lost! It's easy to make: All you have to do is stick sticky notes together. Then accent the cover by adding a cute cat cutout on top!

Instructions → p.67

🐾 Cat Craft 6

Stand-up Cards

This stand-up card can be used to send greetings to family and friends or to accompany a gift. Just imagine the smile on their faces when they open your card and see the inspired, charming greeting you've made them. You can also keep the card for yourself as a decorative element.

Instructions → p.67

❀ Cat Craft 7

Labeled Index Cards

Bring a bit of playfulness to your index cards by sticking your cat cutouts onto them. By using multiple cutouts, you can make your index card collection look like a diorama. You can also use round stickers to help you function and organize whatever you need to: recipes, business cards, and more.

Instructions → p.69

You can also make postcard-size indexes to organize greeting cards.

Variation

Pocket File Folders

Once you've made your sticky kitty index cards, make a skyline for them! Glue envelopes together into an accordion-type file folder collection. Next, cut out a backdrop and glue it to the back of the accordion, then place your sticky kitty index cards into the envelopes to make the files look like a diorama!

Instructions → p.69

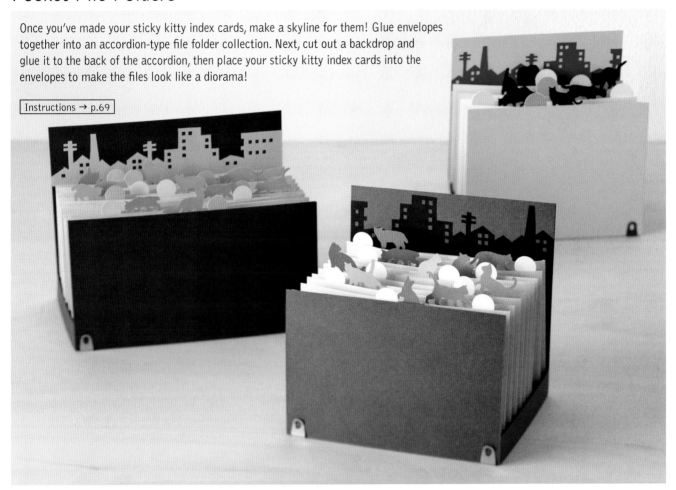

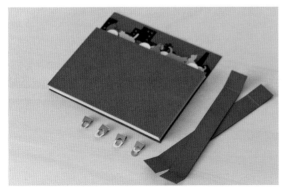

The files can be flattened if you remove the clips used for locking the frames.

You can use envelopes with patterns, such as ones used for airmail, to give the files a lively look.

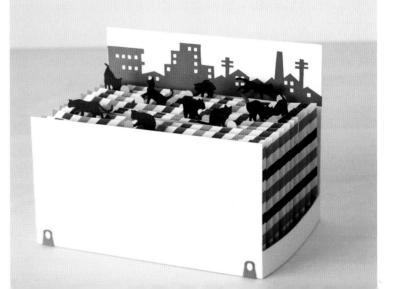

🐾 Cat Craft 8

Pop-up Cards

These cards pop up to reveal a room with cats inside. The sidewalls are adhered to the base with low-tack glue, so you can remove them and fold the cards flat if you like. Once folded, you can mail the cards in an envelope.

Instructions → p.70

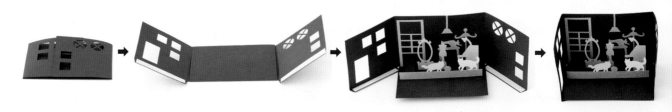

The rooms on the left use solid-color construction paper to make the furniture and cats, creating a color-blocked feel. On the right, the rooms are embellished using ink stamps, postage stamps, and decorative paper. Have fun setting multiple pop-up-card rooms next to each other to create a housing complex!

🐾 Cat Craft 9

Decorative Tape

Make decorative tape using sticky notes that come in rolls. You can stick the tape onto jars and boxes to create a panorama of sticky kitties in action!

Instructions → p.74

You can also stick the tape onto a wall to make a whimsical border.

Variation

Simple Storage Boxes

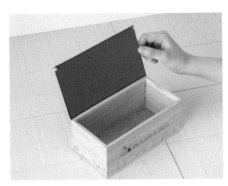

This is a plain storage box made beautiful by adding a cardboard cover and sticky kitty tape. These wooden boxes can be purchased at craft stores.

Instructions → p.74

You can use any combination of printed decorative tapes, ink stamps, postage stamps, and ribbons to decorate your box.

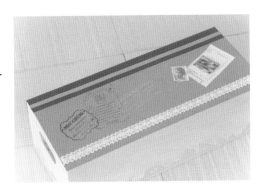

❧ Cat Craft 10

Box Dollhouse

We made dollhouses using partitioned wooden trays, which can be found at craft stores. You might have to make your sticky kitties smaller so you can fit them comfortably in the rooms!

Instructions → p.76

You can keep the dollhouse simple by just making cutouts of furniture and cats. Or you can also add ornaments, postage stamps, and other miniatures to make it more true to life!

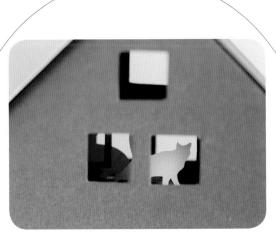

Peekaboo! If you cut out windows for the house, you can catch a glimpse of the cats inside.

You can use masking tape to decorate your furniture cutouts.

🐾 Cat Craft 11

Layered Diorama Cards

These are layered diorama cards show a scene. You can attach your sticky kitties wherever you like and let your cats play around. The cards can be expanded for use as a decoration, then folded up to store. Why don't you try creating original scenery?

Instructions → p.79

These cards can be folded and mailed in an envelope. Everyone wants to receive a personalized scene of sticky kitties as a gift!

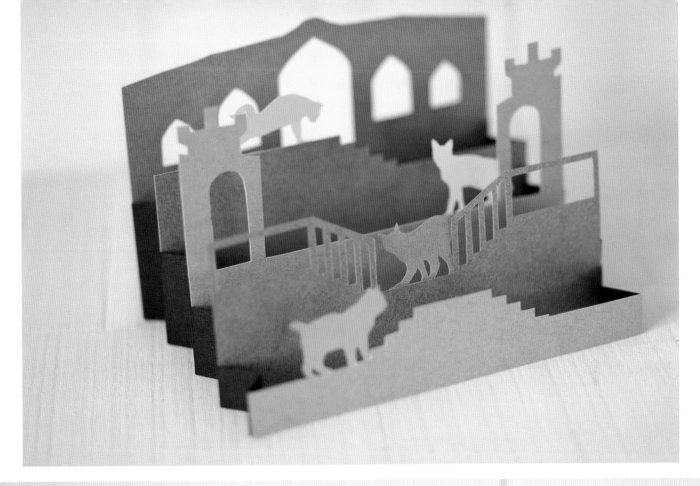

By using single-color construction paper and black-cat cutouts,
you can create a graphic two-tone atmosphere.

Cat Behaviors Explained

There are reasons why cats scratch their necks and yawn.
They're not just casual gestures for cats!

Endearing Cat Gestures

Scratching is not just to relieve itching

Don't you often see cats scratching the back of their necks? Cats clean themselves by licking their coats, but the back of the neck is one place that cats cannot lick, even with their flexible bodies. That is why they have no choice but to use their paws to rub that area.

Cats can't help pouncing on things that move

Cats are curious creatures, and they are particularly interested in things that move. When they see something on the go, they immediately make a beeline for it or pounce on it. Perhaps it brings out their hunting instinct. Yet some cats show no interest in toys at all, no matter how much you shake them!

Yawns are for a change of pace

When cats yawn, they seem to be inhaling large amounts of oxygen to refresh themselves and start anew. But when a snoozing cat yawns while you are petting it, that may be a sign of discomfort. He might be thinking, "This isn't fun. I should skedaddle."

Cat Craft 1 | Cat House Envelopes

Materials & Tools Envelope with a transparent window • Scissors • Glue tape (strong adhesion) • Construction paper • Eyeleteer

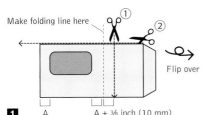

Make folding line here

① ②

Flip over

1 A   A + ⅜ inch (10 mm)

Take an envelope with a window and make a crease at a point where the space on one side of the window is equal to the space on the other side (i.e., length A in diagram above). Cut the envelope at a point ⅜ inch (10 mm) out from the folding line (① in diagram above). Slit open the full length of the top side of the envelope (② in diagram above).

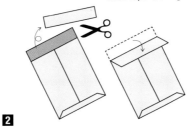

2

Flip the envelope over to show its back. On the edge that was cut in step **1**, cut off just the top layer of the envelope at the crease. Fold the remaining layer and glue it onto the back of the envelope to enclose that edge.

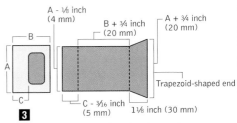

A - ⅛ inch (4 mm)
B + ¾ inch (20 mm)
A + ¾ inch (20 mm)
B
A
C
C - 3⁄16 inch (5 mm)
Trapezoid-shaped end
1⅛ inch (30 mm)

3

To create the insert sheet for the envelope, cut construction paper to the size shown in the diagram above, using the envelope made in step **2** for size comparison. Using an eyeleteer, perforate along the dotted lines shown in the diagram above.

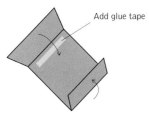

Add glue tape

4

Fold along the dotted lines on the insert sheet made in step **3** and stick down the trapezoid-shaped end using glue tape.

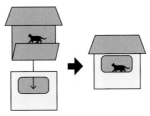

5

Place a sticky kitty on the other folded end of the insert sheet and put the sheet inside the envelope. You have just made your cat house envelope! You can use ink stamps and decorative tape to adorn your package.

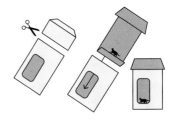

6

To make a tall-house envelope, simply cut the envelope at around ① in the diagram above step **1**, skip step **2**, and continue from step **3** on.

Cat Craft 2 | Gift Bags

Materials & Tools Used postage stamp or memo sheet • Paper bag • Craft knife • Paper fastener • Twist tie • Memo tag, sticker, or label of your choice

Version a

Used postage stamp

1

Cut out a sticky kitty of your choice. Stick a thin paper item, such as a used postage stamp or a memo sheet, on the adhesive part of your cutout.

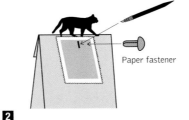

Paper fastener

2

Fold the top of a paper bag, place the decoration you made in step **1** on the upper part of the bag, and use the craft knife to pierce a hole through the decoration and the paper bag. Push a paper fastener through the hole.

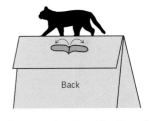

Back

3

Turn the bag around and bend the tines of the fastener outward to attach it to the bag. You have just made an adorable closure for your gift bag!

Version b

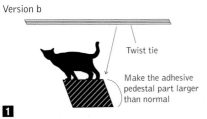

Twist tie

Make the adhesive pedestal part larger than normal

1

To make a gift bag closure using a twist tie, make a larger area for the adhesive pedestal part when cutting out your sticky kitty. Lay the twist tie across the middle of the adhesive area.

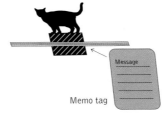

Message

Memo tag

2

Stick a memo tag onto the adhesive part of your cutout. Feel free to use your favorite sticker, label, or other item in place of the tag for variety.

Message

3

Fold the top of a paper bag, place the decoration you made in step **2** on the upper part of the bag, wrap the twist tie around the bag, and twist its ends together.

Cat Craft 3 | Simple Garlands

Materials & Tools Scissors • Craft knife • Cutting mat • Construction paper • Photocopy of patterns below • Decorative tape • Doilies • String • Masking tape

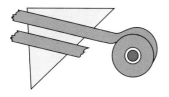

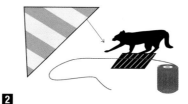

1

Cut construction paper into the shapes below using a photocopy of the patterns (in this example, we use only the triangle). You can also use scrapbooking paper, which comes in countless designs. Decorate the flags with decorative tape or even doilies.

2

Prepare a sticky kitty of your choice and lay a string across the middle of its adhesive area. Place a flag prepared in step **1** onto the adhesive area of the cat cutout, sandwiching the string.

3

As in the diagram above, the cat cutout should sit on top, with the flag serving as the weight beneath.

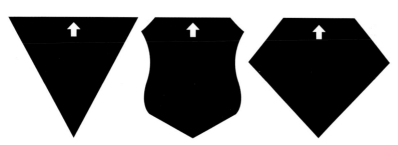

4

Use the same procedure to make many flags, and use sticky kitties to adhere them to the same string. Secure both ends of the string with masking tape to make an enviable garland!

Patterns for Simple Garlands (make 141% enlarged photocopy)

Cat Craft 4 | Cat Hooks

Materials & Tools Photocopy of patterns below • Sticky notes (film-type recommended) • Craft knife • Cutting mat • String or hook

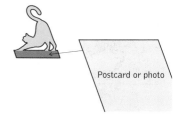

1

Make a full-size photocopy of the patterns below and attach one to a sticky note. We recommend durable film-type sticky notes for this project.

2

Cut along the outline of the pattern, in the same way you'd cut out regular sticky notes.

3

Stick a postcard, photo, cute business card, etc. onto the adhesive part of your cutout.

Patterns for Cat Hooks (make full-size photocopy)

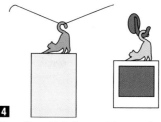

4

Hang the cat's tail on a string or a hook to create an adorable cat hook.

Cat Craft 5 | Sticky-Note Covers

Materials & Tools Sticky notes • Glue tape (strong adhesion and low-tack) • Scissors • Craft knife • Cutting mat • Origami paper

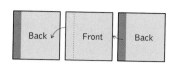

1

Connect three 3-x-3-inch (75-x-75-mm) sticky notes. As in the diagram above, stick them together using the adhesive on the edges.

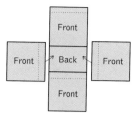

2

Flip over the three connected sticky notes. Then, connect two more 3-x-3-inch (75-x-75-mm) sticky notes to the set you connected in step **1**, one on each side.

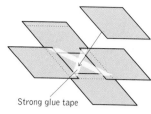

Strong glue tape

3

To securely attach the side flaps, apply strong glue tape onto the center area of the combined sticky notes and paste another sticky note over the glue tape.

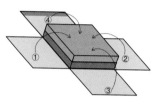

4

Stack some sticky-note pads on the center and fold over the sides in the order indicated in the diagram above.

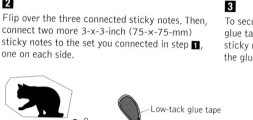

Low-tack glue tape

5

Prepare a sticky kitty from a pattern of your choice and cut off the pedestal part. Stick the pattern onto origami paper using low-tack glue.

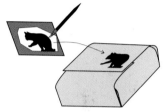

6

Cut out the cat, apply glue to its back, and paste it on the sticky note cover as a delightful adornment.

Cat Craft 6 | Stand-up Cards

Materials & Tools Photocopy of patterns on p. 68 • Glue tape (low-tack and strong adhesion) • Construction paper • Craft knife • Cutting mat • Eyeleteer

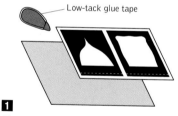

Low-tack glue tape

1

Photocopy the patterns on p. 68 and glue them onto construction paper using low-tack glue tape.

2

Cut out the patterns with a craft knife. Then, use an eyeleteer to perforate along the dotted line in the diagram above.

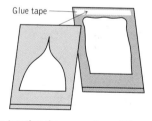

Glue tape

3

Paste together the upper edges of the cutout patterns using strong glue tape. Fold in the perforated parts.

4

Prepare a sticky kitty of your choice and paste it on the stand-up card as shown.

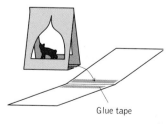

Glue tape

5

Cut a 7⅞-x-3-inch (200-x-75-mm) rectangle of construction paper. Fold it in half and then open it up again. Apply strong glue tape along the crease and paste the bottom of your stand-up card onto the tape.

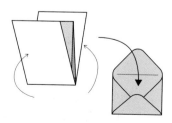

6

Try folding and unfolding the completed card to make sure it works. When folded, you can put it in an envelope and mail it!

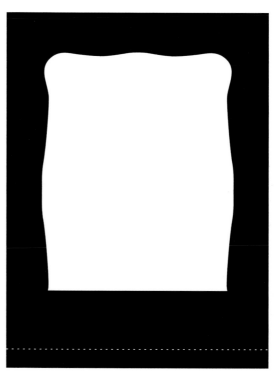

Patterns for Stand-up Cards (make full-size photocopy)

Cat Craft 7 | Labeled Index Cards

Materials & Tools Construction paper • Index card or cardstock • Round stickers (large) • Craft knife • Cutting mat • Glue tape (strong adhesion)

1 Make a cat-shaped cutout using construction paper or any other paper of your choice and paste it onto an index card (or a piece of cardstock cut to your preferred size) with glue tape. Refer to p. 32 for instructions on how to make sticky-note cutouts using plain, nonsticky paper.

2 Take two large, round stickers and stick them together, partly sandwiching the index card. You can use the sticker as a category label by writing or stamping letters or numbers on it.

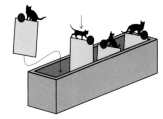

3 Make more cards as necessary and insert them in a box to categorize whatever you put inside.

Variation | Pocket File Folders

Materials & Tools Envelopes • Heavy cardstock • Origami paper • Scissors • Craft knife • Cutting mat • Glue tape (both strong adhesion and low-tack) • Cardboard • Photocopy of pattern on p. 73 • 4 sturdy clips

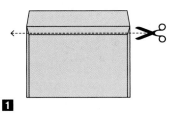

1 Prepare about 10 envelopes by cutting off the flaps on all of them.

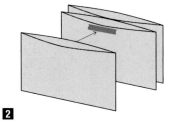

2 Apply strong glue tape on the outside of the envelope, on the middle near the cut edge. This allows the envelopes to stick together in a stack that can stretch out like an accordion.

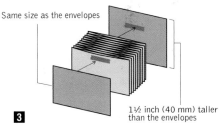

Same size as the envelopes

1½ inch (40 mm) taller than the envelopes

3 As in the diagram above, cut the heavy cardstock into two rectangles and glue them onto the front and back of the stack of envelopes made in step **2**.

Low-tack glue tape

4 Stick a photocopy of the city silhouette on p. 73 onto a sheet of origami paper using low-tack glue tape. Cut out the pattern using a craft knife to create the background design.

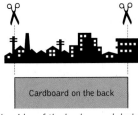

Cardboard on the back

5 Cut the sides of the background design to match the width of the cardboard on the back of the envelope stack.

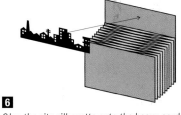

6 Glue the city silhouette onto the heavy cardstock.

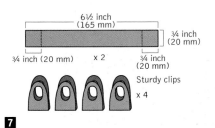

6½ inch (165 mm)

¾ inch (20 mm)

¾ inch (20 mm) x 2 ¾ inch (20 mm)

Sturdy clips x 4

7 To create the frames, cut the heavy cardstock into two long rectangles as shown in the diagram above. Prepare four sturdy clips.

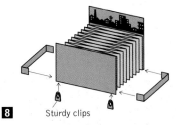

Sturdy clips

8 Attach the frames made in step **7** onto the envelope stack made in step **6** as shown in the diagram above. Fold the edges of the rectangles to fit them into place, then secure the frames by using the sturdy clips.

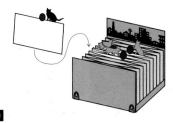

9 Create index cards that fit the envelopes and insert them inside.

Cat Craft 8 | Pop-up Cards

Materials & Tools Photocopy of patterns on pp. 71–73 • Construction paper • Glue tape (low-tack and strong adhesion) • Scissors • Craft knife • Cutting mat • Eyeleteer • Double-sided tape • Sticky-note tape roll

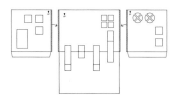

1

Photocopy the patterns on p. 72 and the left side of p. 73, and connect them with glue by overlapping the gray areas as shown above.

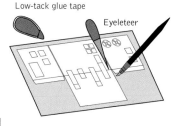

2

Paste the connected patterns onto a sheet of construction paper using low-tack glue tape, and cut out the pattern using a craft knife. Use an eyeleteer to perforate the folding lines.

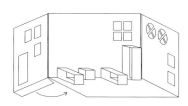

3

Fold the pattern by mountain fold or valley fold as indicated on the patterns. This will serve as the base for your pop-up card.

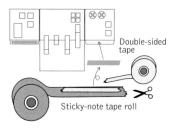

4

Attach double-sided tape to a sticky-note tape roll and cut it with scissors to fit the length of the two areas indicated by the shaded rectangles in the diagram above. Then stick the tape in those spots.

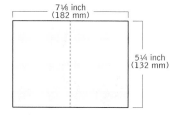

5

To make a cover, cut construction paper of the same color as the paper used in step **2** to the size indicated in the above diagram.

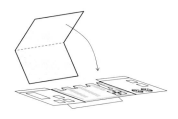

6

Fold over the base made in step **3** as in the diagram above, and paste the cover on it with glue tape.

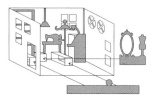

7

Assemble the pop-up base and make cutouts of furniture using the patterns on p. 71. Paste the cutouts onto appropriate parts of the base using glue tape or other adhesives. Refer to the numbers on the patterns.

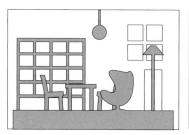

Refer to the photographs on pp. 56–57 and the diagrams above for ideas on where to paste furniture cutouts.

8

Place sticky kitties of your choice onto the base.

9

Detach the sides of the base and neatly fold the pop-up card.

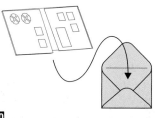

10

You can put the folded card in an envelope and mail it!

Patterns for Pop-up Cards
(make full-size photocopy)

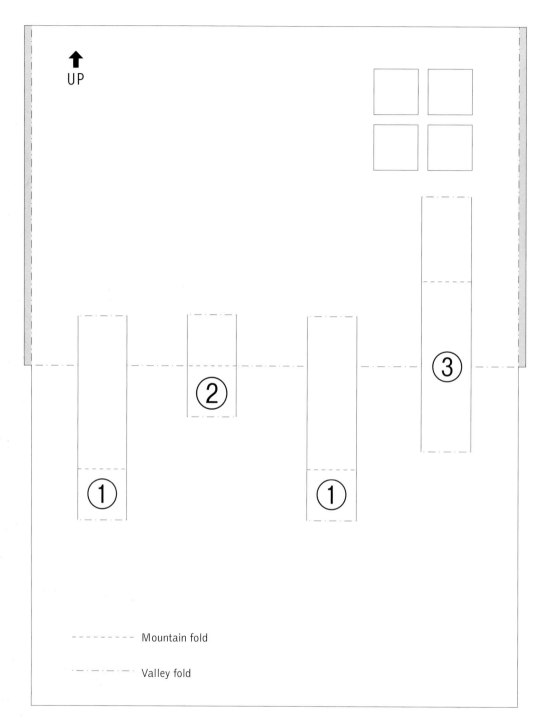

UP

③

②

① ①

-------- Mountain fold

-·-·-·-· Valley fold

Pattern for Pop-up Cards (make full-size photocopy)

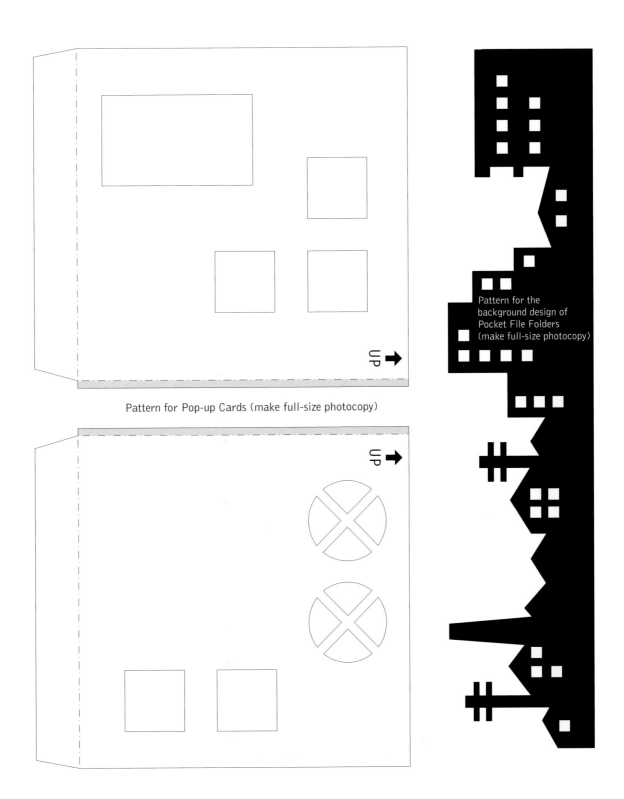

UP ➡

Pattern for Pop-up Cards (make full-size photocopy)

UP ➡

Pattern for the background design of Pocket File Folders (make full-size photocopy)

Cat Craft 9 | Decorative Tape

Materials & Tools Photocopy of patterns on p. 75 • Craft knife • Cutting mat • Magic transparent tape • Sticky-note tape roll (strong adhesion)

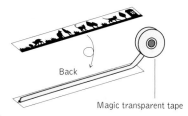

Back

Magic transparent tape

1
Photocopy the patterns on p. 75 and cut them out along the rectangular outlines. Stick magic transparent tape across the back of the patterns.

Sticky-note tape roll

2
Adhere the sticky-note tape to the backs of the patterns. We recommend sticky-note tape rolls with strong adhesive glue for better attachment.

3
Cut out the patterns with a craft knife, leaving the black areas intact.

Peel upward starting from the base

4
Peel off the pattern slowly. Start from the base and peel upward little by little.

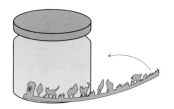

5
Attach the cutout onto items such as a jar or box.

6
You can increase the length of the cutout by connecting the cutout patterns.

Variation | Simple Storage Boxes

Materials & Tools Wooden box • Cardboard • Scissors • Craft knife • Cutting mat • Bookbinding tape • Decorative cutout tape • Ink stamps • Printed tape

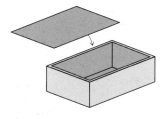

1
Find a small wooden box (available at craft stores). Cut cardboard to a size that fits the opening of the box to act as a lid.

Bookbinding tape

2
Place the cardboard on top of the box and attach half the width of bookbinding tape to a side edge of the cardboard.

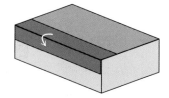

3
To finish the cover for the box, fold the bookbinding tape onto the side of the box to connect it with the cardboard.

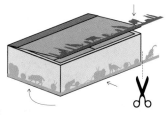

4
Stick the decorative cutout tape onto the box and its cover. If the decorative tape is too long, cut it to fit the length of the box.

5
You can also use ink stamps and printed tape to decorate the box.

Patterns for Decorative Tape (make 141% enlarged photocopy)

Cat Craft 10 | Box Dollhouse

Materials & Tools: Partitioned wooden trays • Heavy cardstock • Cardstock • Utility knife • Craft knife • Cutting mat • Eyeleteer • Glue tape (strong adhesion and low-tack) • Double-sided tape • Pencil • Bookbinding tape • Measuring tape • Photocopy of patterns on pp. 77–78

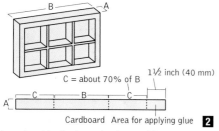

B — A
C = about 70% of B
1½ inch (40 mm)
C   B   C
A
Cardboard   Area for applying glue

1
Purchase two identical wooden trays with partitions (craft stores should have a good selection). Measure the sides of the trays, and cut cardboard into the size shown in the diagram above.

Apply glue tape here

2
Use an eyeleteer to perforate the dotted lines on the cardboard in the diagram for step **1**, and fold it at the lines. Apply strong glue tape on the area indicated in the diagram above, and press down to form a triangular shape.

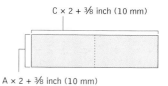

C × 2 + ⅜ inch (10 mm)
A × 2 + ⅜ inch (10 mm)

3
To create the roof, cut another piece of cardboard in the size indicated in the diagram. Perforate the dotted line with an eyeleteer. We recommend you choose a complementary color that will stand out.

Double-sided tape

4
For a steady fit, attach the triangular part made in step **2** firmly onto the top of the wooden trays using double-sided tape.

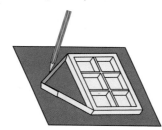

5
Place the dollhouse made in step **4** onto cardboard and trace its outline with a pencil. Repeat the task on another piece of cardboard.

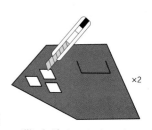

×2

6
Use a utility knife to cut along the outline drawn on the two pieces of heavy cardstock. Cut out small squares for windows in appropriate places in the upper triangular area, and create a door near the bottom by cutting three sides of a rectangular shape, as in the above diagram.

Bookbinding tape

7
Place the dollhouse made in step **4** and the other tray next to each other, with the partitioned sides facing each other. Connect the two trays on one side with bookbinding tape.

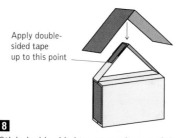

Apply double-sided tape up to this point

8
Stick double-sided tape onto the top of the triangular piece. Important: On the side of the triangle next to the bookbinding tape, apply the double-sided tape only to the upper half; on the other side of the triangle, apply double-sided tape to the whole length. Press the roof made in step **3** to the top of the tape.

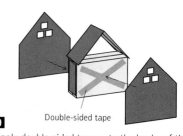

Double-sided tape

9
Apply double-sided tape onto the backs of the trays, as in the diagram above, and stick on the pieces made in step **6**.

10
Lift the roof slightly on the side with the bookbinding tape and open the trays sideways to show the inside of the house.

11
Photocopy the patterns on p. 77 and make cutouts of the furniture using cardstock. Attach the furniture cutouts to the interior of the house using glue tape (strong adhesion and low-tack).

12
Finally, use the patterns on p. 78 to make sticky kitties. Place them throughout the house. You can also add ornaments, miniature items, and used postage stamps for decoration.

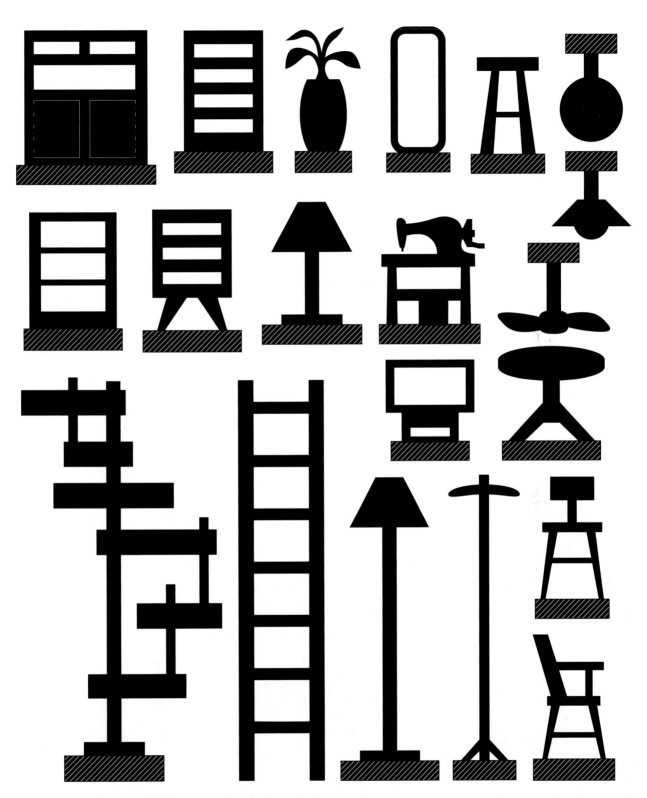

Patterns for Box Dollhouse (make full-size photocopy)

These are for use in the Box Dollhouse. They can also be used for other crafts, such as Pop-up Cards and Pocket File Folders, when you need smaller cat cutouts. (make full-size photocopy)

Materials & Tools: Photocopy of patterns on pp. 80–81 • Cardstock • Glue tape (low-tack and strong adhesion) • Craft knife • Cutting mat • Origami paper • Eyeleteer • Utility knife

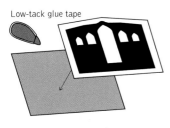

1
Photocopy the patterns on p. 81 and stick them onto cardstock using low-tack glue tape.

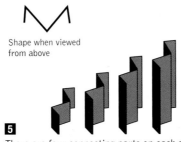

2
Use a craft knife to cut out the patterns.

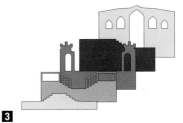

3
When you have cut out all five main parts, stack them in the order of the numbers printed on the patterns. We recommend you use a different color for each part, but using the same color for all of them is also fine.

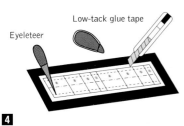

4
Take the photocopy of the pattern for the connecting parts on p. 81 and stick it on origami paper. Perforate the dotted lines with an eyeleteer. Cut the solid lines with a utility knife.

5
There are four connecting parts on each side, for a total of eight parts. Fold the eight parts by alternating a mountain fold and valley fold. The parts should be M-shaped when viewed from above.

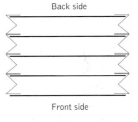

6
Stick the shortest connecting parts onto the back side of the main part numbered ① using strong glue tape, as shown in the diagram above.

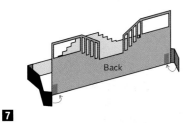

7
Wrap the unattached end of the connecting parts from step **6** onto the back of the main part numbered ②. Attach them with strong glue tape.

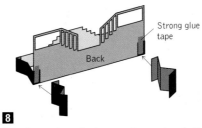

8
Take the next smallest connecting part and stick its end onto the back of what was made in step **7**, overlapping with the ends of the smallest connecting part. Repeat steps **6** through **8** to attach the remaining parts.

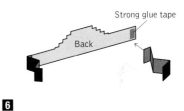

9
The layered parts should look like this from above. Try to make the connecting parts as invisible as possible when looking from the front side.

10
Decorate the diorama with sticky kitties of your choice. Smaller cat cutouts should fit in better.

11
You can fold the layered diorama card and send it inside an envelope. For the patterns on p. 80, follow the same procedures to make a layered diorama card with different scenery.

Patterns for Layered Diorama Cards
(make 141% enlarged photocopy)

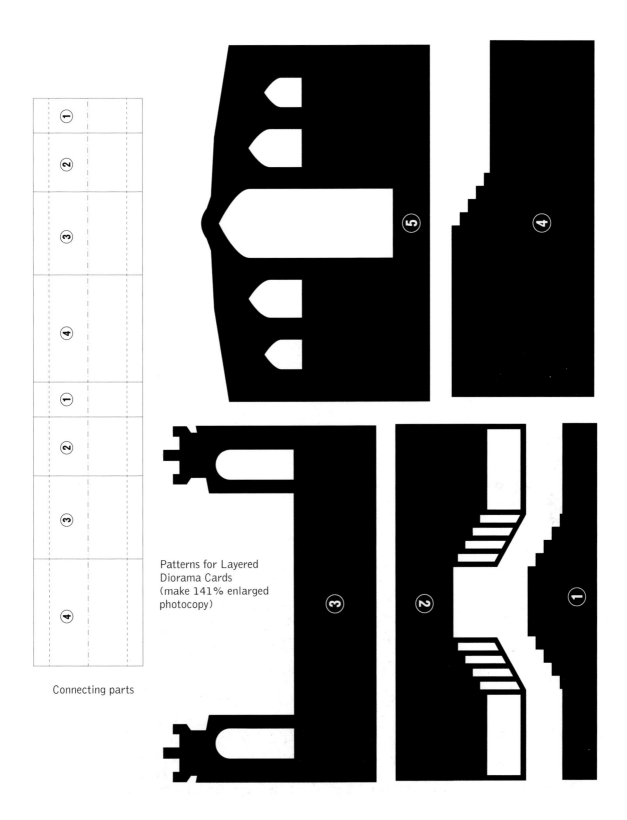

Connecting parts

Patterns for Layered
Diorama Cards
(make 141% enlarged
photocopy)

Patterns for
Sticky Kitty Cutouts (make full-size photocopy)

The patterns on pp. 82–93 are for making cat-shaped and other sticky-note cutouts. You can start with making full-size photocopies, but if you find them too small for the intricate cutting required, try working with 120% enlarged photocopies. For use in the crafts in chapter 3, we recommend you make reduced photocopies.

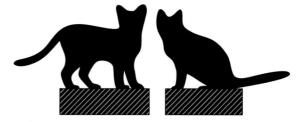

Basic patterns: Try making cutouts of these first.

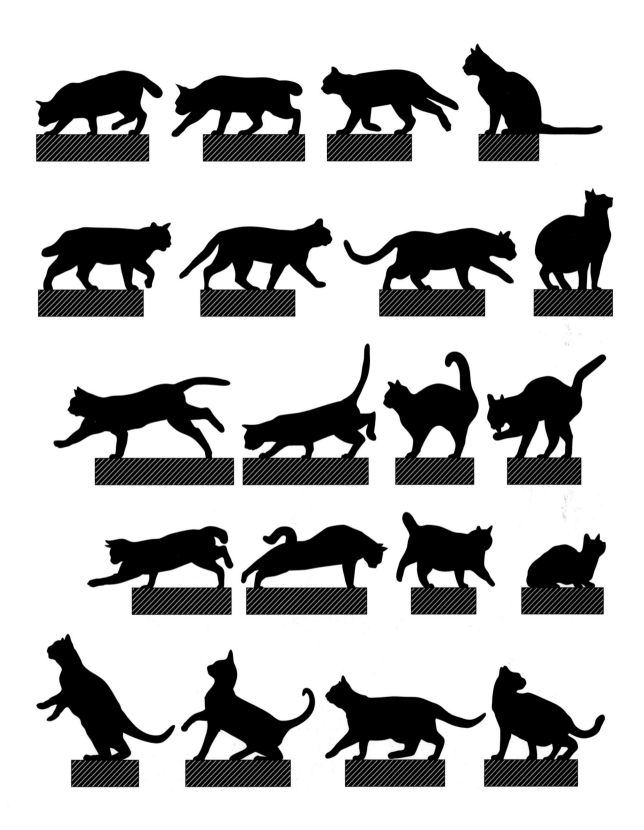

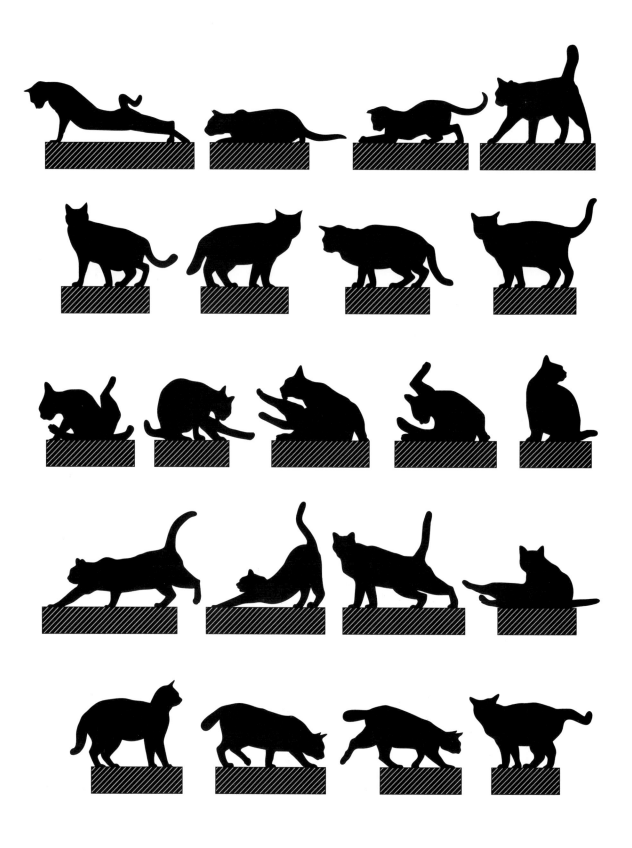

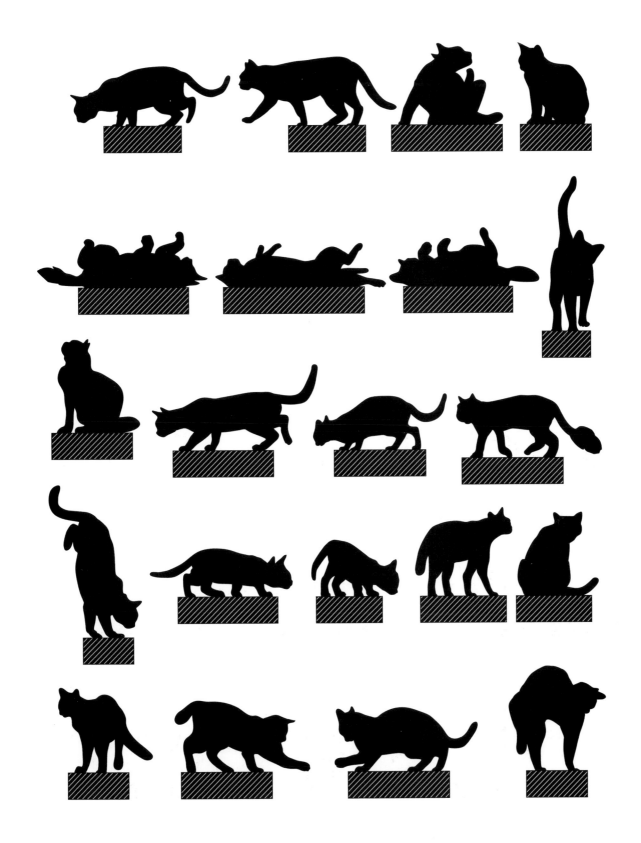

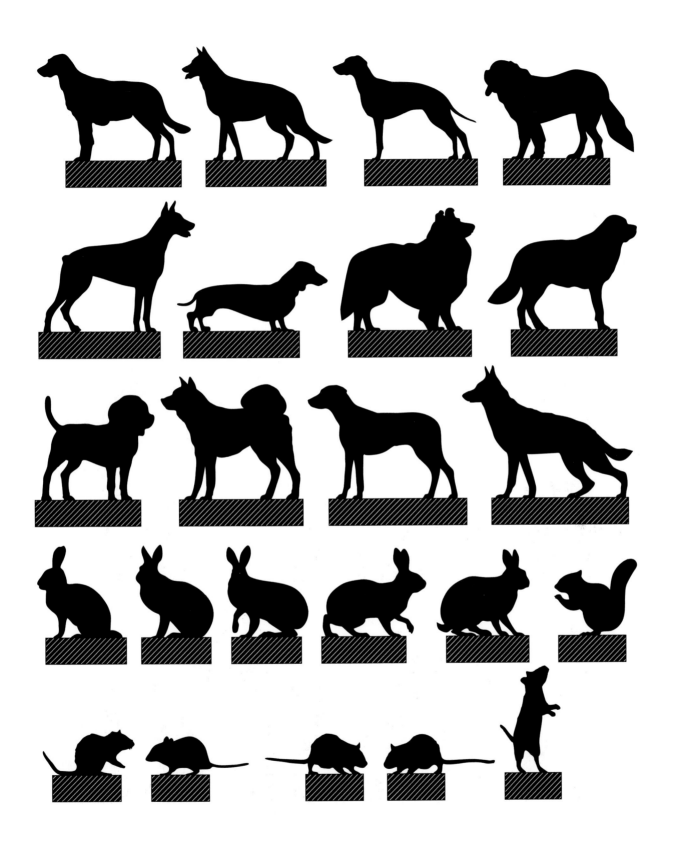

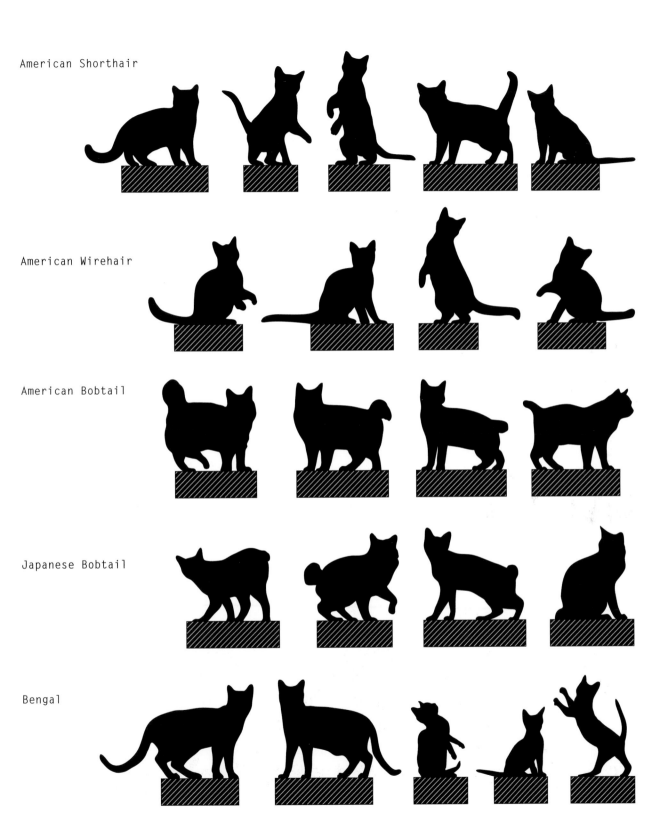

American Shorthair

American Wirehair

American Bobtail

Japanese Bobtail

Bengal

89

British Shorthair

Persian

Ocicat

Burmese

Scottish Fold

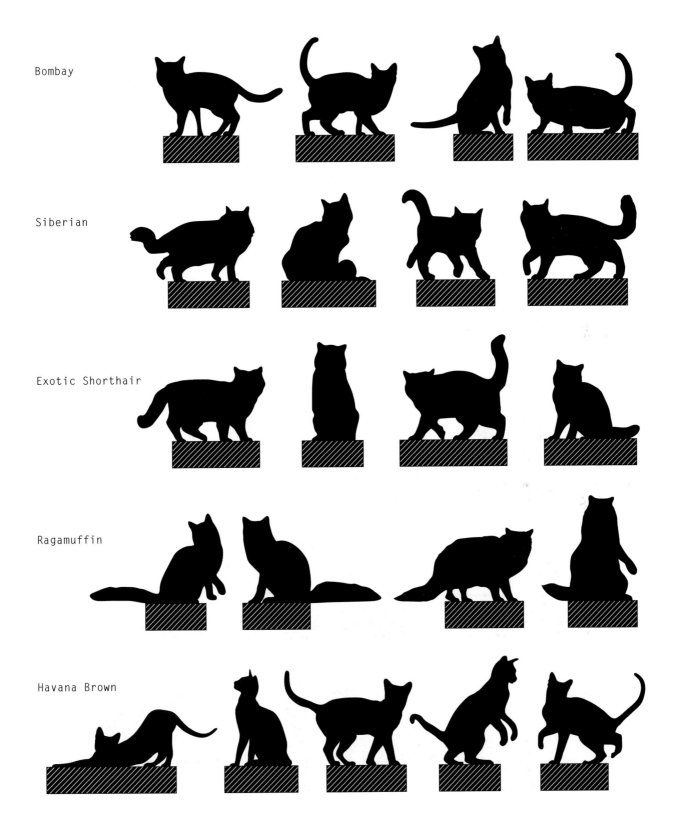

Bombay

Siberian

Exotic Shorthair

Ragamuffin

Havana Brown

91

Norwegian Forest Cat

Ragdoll

Russian Blue

Chartreux

Oriental

Cornish Rex

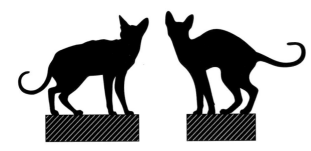

Turkish Angora

Abyssinian

Birman

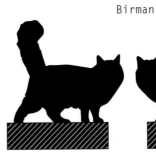 

Siamese

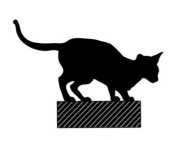 

Singapura

Maine Coon

Somali

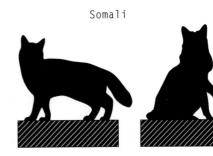

BLOG

"Dakara Tokyo ga Suki! Machi no Nekotachi"

(The Reason I Love Tokyo! Cats Around Town)

http://cats-blog.com/

We asked the author of this Japanese blog to write the text and provide material for the cat patterns. His blog shows photographs of various poses, behaviors, and expressions of cats around town. The blog's narrative photographs make you feel like you're watching the world from the eyes of a cat.

Administrator: **kiyochan**

Profile

Born in Tokyo in 1958, Kiyochan has been taking photos of cats in Tokyo for more than a decade. His hobby became his career when he quit his job in 2011 to become a freelance photographer. Every day, he looks for opportunities to take snapshots of cats somewhere in Tokyo.

Special Thanks

Sumitomo 3M Ltd.
2-33-1 Tamagawadai, Setagaya-ku, Tokyo, Japan
☎ +81-(0)3-3709-8165
www.mmm.co.jp

Vision Quest Co. Ltd.
2F 2-18-9 Shinmachi, Nishi-ku, Osaka, Japan
☎ +81-(0)6-6536-5877
www.vq-goods.com

Yamato Co. Ltd.
9-10 Nihonbashi Odenmacho, Chuo-ku, Tokyo, Japan
☎ +81-(0)3-3662-7456
www.yamato.co.jp

Toyo Corp.
2-12-12 Senju Midoricho, Adachi-ku, Tokyo, Japan
☎ +81-(0)3-3888-7821
www.kidstoyo.co.jp

Tombow Pencil Co. Ltd.
6-10-12 Toshima, Kita-ku, Tokyo, Japan
☎ 0120-834198 (Toll-free in Japan)
www.tombow.com

Tools Corp.
3-38-1 Shinjuku, Shinjuku-ku, Tokyo, Japan
☎ +81-(0)3-3352-7437
www.tools-shop.jp

Profile

Killigraph

Killigraph is the brand name of editorial designer Takuji Segawa. He mainly plans the editorial design for books and magazines, and also engages in editing. Since 2007, he has put out Killigraph Sticky Notes, which are sticky-note cutout creations, and Archi Killigraph works, which involve making miniature architecture using paper cutouts as part of the Killigraph Project. He has also written many books.

Books Written
Antiku Kirie Sutairu (Asukashinsha Publishing)
Fusen de Tsukuru Minichua Kirie (Boutique-sha)
Fusen de Tsukuru 1/40 no Sekai (Seishun Publishing)
Chiisakute Kawaii! Disney no Fusen Kirie (Boutique-sha)

Books Co-written
Otayori Techo, written and edited by Killigraph
(Tokyo Chizu Publishing)
Kawaii Rappingu Sozai BOOK, written by Hello
Sandwich, Kyou, and Killigraph (Gijutsu-Hyohron)

Fusen de Neko Craft
by Killigraph

Copyright © 2013 Killigraph and Graphic-sha Publishing Co., Ltd.

This book was first designed and published in Japan in 2013 by Graphic-sha Publishing Co., Ltd.

This English-language edition was published in 2014 by Weldon Owen Inc.

Weldon Owen, Inc. is a division of Bonnier Corporation
415 Jackson Street, San Francisco, CA 94111

Library of Congress Cataloging-in-Publication data is available.
ISBN 13: 978-1-61628-805-1
ISBN 10: 1-61628-805-1
www.weldonowen.com

Printed and bound in China by Everbest Printing
First US printing: July 2014
10 9 8 7 6 5 4 3 2 1

Staff
Design and Editing: Takuji Segawa (Killigraph)
Photography: Boco
Photography Assistant: Sachiko Ito
Cat Behaviors' Photographs and text: Kiyochan
Editorial Assistance: Tomoko Yabe
Planning and Editing: Kumiko Sakamoto (Graphic-sha Publishing)

English edition creative staff
English translation: Sarah Suk
Layout: Shinichi Ishioka
Production: Kumiko Sakamoto (Graphic-sha Publishing)

Reference Literature
Sekai no Neko Zukan, editorial supervision by Yayoi Sato (Shinsei Publishing)
Sekai no Neko Tachi, commentary by Gloria Stephens, photography by Tetsu Yamazaki (Yama-kei Publishers)

Reference URL
Nyanderful www.nyanderful.biz